CAREERS IN THE

RAILROAD INDUSTRY

THE TIME TO CHOOSE A CAREER IS AN exciting time. Your career will define many parts of your life for years to come. You owe it to yourself to give this decision the attention it deserves.

Some careers are essential. They may not be glamorous or lead to fame and fortune, but the world would not be able to get along without them. Railroading is one of those careers. When many people think of railroading they think of old-fashioned steam locomotives, streamlined passenger trains from times gone by or maybe pages from a school history book. Railroads have played a role in the development of the United States, and are part of our common heritage and lore. They are not as visible as they used to be, with most long-distance passenger travel shifting to airplanes decades ago, and trucks handling a large proportion of cross-country hauling. The truth is railroads are as important as they ever were.

Railroads are the least-expensive way to haul heavy loads over long distances on land. Trains use thousands of miles of dedicated right-of-way to travel long distances around the clock using only a handful of operators. In a typical day American railroads deliver more than five million tons of consumer and industrial goods to cities across the country, and play a vital role in the container shipping system that moves goods around the world. Railroads deliver about 70 percent of all the coal used in the United States. Looked at another way, railroads provide nearly 40 percent of the electricity used in the United States by carrying the coal necessary to generate it. It would be hard to name another industry more essential to the American economy.

Perhaps ironically, employment in the railroad industry is expected to shrink in the coming decades. This has nothing to do with railroading's importance or even with demand for its services, but rather with its suitability for technological transformation. Many of the jobs once done by people, like switching and even engineering, are being taken over by computers that can do the job just as well for a lot less money. People will never be completely factored out of the railroading equation, however, and the jobs that remain are more challenging and rewarding than they have ever been.

Take careful note of the information contained in this report. In it you will find sections on how to prepare for your career, from what kind of education and training you will need to how to get a little experience in railroading right now. You will also find sections on how much money you can expect to earn at various stages in your career, what you can do to move up the ladder, and even what you may like and dislike about the career. If you like what you read here, keep going! Be sure to check out the links on the last page of this report.

WHAT YOU CAN DO NOW

YOU CAN START ON YOUR CAREER IN the railroad industry right now. Read up on the business and its abundant lore. There is no faster, easier way to learn the ins and outs of a particular industry than by reading the trade journals devoted to it. Business-specific publications and websites cater to a specialist audience and feature articles and news items that cover their industry in much greater depth than ordinary publications. Even the advertising helps to shine a light on the business. Publications devoted to railroading include *Trains, Classic Trains, Railways Illustrated,* and *Modern Railways.* Websites include Sterling Rail, Train Web, and Railroad Data.

Model railroading may not be railroading but the hobby has endured for so long because it is fun and a great way to learn the basics of railroading. Even a simple layout will teach you a thing or two about switching, and an elaborate layout can include as much detail as you want it to. Most importantly, model railroading will build and maintain your enthusiasm for your eventual career in actual railroading.

Aspiring careerists can get some experience in many careers by getting a part-time job in the field or connecting with a working professional who is willing to show them around. Getting hands-on experience in railroading can be difficult. Common sense, union work rules, and many, many laws make hanging around the rail yard impossible. Rail yards are dangerous places where guests need to be closely supervised. The best way to get involved is through The National Railway Historical Society, which sponsors a weeklong program called RailCamp that gives high school students an opportunity to gain first-hand experience in the railroad industry. During the week students delve into the inner workings of modern railroads and learn about railroading's glorious history. The program is costly. Tuition is about $1300, not including transportation to Wilmington, Delaware or Tacoma, Washington, the only places the program is offered.

HISTORY OF THE CAREER

NO OTHER INDUSTRY IS AS CLOSELY associated with the growth of the United States. Without railroads it would have been much more difficult to move people and goods across the vast expanse of the West. Railroads made entire industries possible, especially cattle ranching and coal mining, both of which are indispensable parts of the larger American economy.

It sounds unlikely, but the first railroads were created as a way to reduce friction. Carriage wheels pulled on uneven ground encounter a great deal of friction, making it difficult to pull heavy loads over long distances. The earliest railroads were not really railroads the way we understand them today, but short tracks with smooth rails and wagons specially sized to ride upon them. Horses pulled the wagons easily due to the relatively low friction from the rails. Known as wagonways or tramways, these small railroads were most often used at quarries or other industrial sites that required a facility to move very heavy loads.

Scottish inventor James Watt patented the first steam locomotive in 1784. An improvement of an earlier design by Thomas Newcomen that had been used to pump water out of mines, the new steam engine was relatively small by the standards of the day, but powerful enough to carry a heavy load. The first true railroad was constructed in Wales in 1804 by Richard Trevithick, an engineer.

The United States was in need of a reliable means to transport passengers and goods over long distances. American John Stevens was granted permission to build the first North American railroad in 1815. He did not get around to firing up his first locomotive until 1826, and his New Jersey Railroad Company was not operational until 1832. As his successors would also discover, building a railroad is an expensive and time-consuming business.

The first railroads were largely purpose-built enterprises meant to service a very specific need. Common-carrier railroads that maintained regular schedules and could haul pretty much anything arrived in 1827 with the founding of the Baltimore and Ohio Railroad, better known as the B&O. The B&O was a huge success, linking up with other railroads throughout the East Coast and ushering in a new era of transportation among the major cities of the day. The railroad was so important to the densely populated Northeast Corridor that it became a favorite target of Confederate forces during the Civil War.

President Abraham Lincoln signed the Pacific Railway Bill in 1862, early in the Civil War. The goal was to link both sides of the continent with a transcontinental railroad able to move large numbers of people and goods across the wide-open plains. The Union Pacific Railroad started laying track at Council Bluffs, Iowa, while the Central

Pacific Railroad laid track beginning in Sacramento, Calif. After laying 1,907 miles of track between them, the two railroads met at Promontory Point, Utah on May 10, 1869. Workers drove a golden spike into the last rail, linking East and West forever.

Demand for rail transport grew rapidly. Consider that in 1840 there were only about 2,800 miles of track in the country. By 1850 there were more than 9,000. By 1870, five years after the end of the Civil War, there were more than 52,000 miles of track laid in the United States. By 1900 the figure had climbed to more than 190,000 miles of track. Mileage peaked in 1916 at 254,000.

Railroads made it possible to open the West to the masses. Spur lines and regional railroads built to connect to the transcontinental railroad served specific markets on the newly settled plains. The cattle industry, for example, actually grew alongside the railroad. In Kansas, the cities of Abilene, Newton, Ellsworth, Wichita and Dodge City, each reigned as a major cattle market for a few years, with each town giving up the title as the railroad headed west, closer to the source of Texas longhorns.

While railroads opened up the dusty West, they also became the favored mode of transportation between cities. Passenger cars that ranged from practical to opulent enabled more people than ever before to travel long distances fairly quickly. By the early 20th century passenger trains had grown into glorious, streamlined Art Deco masterpieces equipped with luxuries like dining cars and observation decks. People often dressed up to ride the train!

Passenger traffic began to wane during the 1930s. Automobiles had become cheap and reliable, and many people used them for long-distance travel. Freight traffic remained important, however. To this day, nobody has come up with a better, cheaper way to move heavy loads over long distances on land.

The railroad industry went into a decline after World War II. Passenger traffic dropped off even more when air travel became common and enabled people to cross the country in hours rather than days. Full-service railroads that carried both passengers and freight scrambled to reorganize their operations. Big railroads bought out smaller railroads in a wave of mergers and consolidations. Things got so bad that in 1970 the federal government passed the Rail Passenger Service Act, bringing almost all of the country's remaining passenger railroads together into a publicly subsidized corporation. The resulting passenger railroad, known as Amtrak, debuted in 1971. In 1976 many freight lines were also consolidated into a government-run corporation known as Conrail. The Staggers Act, passed in 1980 and named for the member of Congress who sponsored it, deregulated much of the railroad industry and allowed railroads to restructure without interference. Reflecting the great disparity between demand for passenger services and demand for freight services, Conrail was sold to private investors in 1987 while Amtrak continues to run essentially all passenger services in the United States to this day.

Today's railroad industry faces an unexpected problem. The decline of passenger rail, along with mergers and consolidations among freight lines, led to a severe reduction in track mileage, from a high of 254,000 in 1916 to about 160,000 today. Although passenger rail today is limited to commuter rail systems in major metropolitan areas and approximately 300 daily Amtrak trains, demand for freight rail has increased enough in recent years to put a strain on the existing system. This is good news for someone like you. Even with automation replacing many jobs of the past, the future of freight rail is assured and expanding.

WHERE YOU WILL WORK

RAILROADS ARE EVERYWHERE. EVERY major city has at least one railroad hub, and maybe several. Many also have passenger rail stations serving local commuter systems and long-haul Amtrak trains. While it is true that big cities are home to the majority of the opportunities, the nature of the railroad business says you ought to be able to work just about anywhere.

First, you need to decide what kind of railroad job you want. Some railroad jobs will allow you to come home at the end of your shift, while others will not. If your goal is to work in a rail yard you will probably go to work and come home like most other people. If you plan to work as a locomotive engineer, conductor, or in some other position that requires you to ride the trains regularly, you may have to leave home for a few days at a time.

Legally, train crews may not work for more than 12 hours at a time. Most crews have a home terminal and an away terminal. They start their journey from their home terminal, travel to an away terminal usually about 200 to 300 miles away, and switch places with a new crew. The original crew then spends the night in a hotel before catching another train. They may turn around and go right home, or catch a train heading in a different direction. Sometimes crews have to be picked up by crew vans and driven home. The point is, if you choose a career that involves riding the trains you will spend time away from home.

DESCRIPTION OF WORK DUTIES

Locomotive Engineers

Locomotive engineers drive trains, a very difficult job. Trains can be a mile long, or even more, and carry millions of pounds of freight. It takes many miles to bring them up to speed and almost as many to bring them to a complete stop. Driving a train is an enormous responsibility. Like pilots or ship captains, locomotive engineers are responsible for their trains.

Locomotive engineers need to be technically savvy. The cab on a modern diesel-electric locomotive looks like the instrument panel on a fighter plane. It is filled with switches and gauges, all of which have important functions. Engineers need to be able to read their panel at a glance in order to make sure that the locomotive is working properly. Diesel-electric locomotives are incredibly reliable and can run for millions of miles with only routine maintenance, but that maintenance needs to be done according to strict procedures. Engineers are not mechanics, but they are usually the first to notice when something is going wrong.

Locomotive engineers need to be keenly aware of what they are pulling and what kind of track they will encounter during a trip. An engineer pulling hazardous chemicals, for example, must be especially careful to leave plenty of time for braking. All engineers need to drive slowly when there is a chance of encountering ice on the rails.

Staying in touch with dispatchers is very important to locomotive engineers. Schedules can change while a train is in motion. Sometimes trains have to be switched to another track unexpectedly, or even diverted to another destination. Engineers need to stay in constant contact with dispatchers and keep a close eye on signals along the track to make sure they know what is up ahead.

Rail Yard Engineers

Sometimes known as hostlers, rail yard engineers drive dinkey locomotives around yards to move rolling stock and locomotives into position to form trains. Rail yard engineers take their orders from yardmasters who are responsible for the big picture.

Rail yard engineers also move full-sized locomotives around yards so they can be hitched to trains. They also move locomotives and other rolling stock in and out of maintenance shops and generally make sure that all the components of trains are where they need to be when they need to be there. Rail yard engineers sometimes climb the ladder to become locomotive engineers or yardmasters.

Conductors

Most people think of conductors as the smiling customer-service professionals who take tickets and answer questions about train schedules. This is only partly correct. Conductors do indeed provide customer service on commuter lines and long-haul Amtrak trains. They are often the only railroad employees with whom customers have any real interaction.

Conductors spend most of their time, however, attending to business that the customers never see. Conductors manage trains. They supervise all of the other employees on the train, manage onloading and offloading of freight, baggage and mail, make announcements to passengers and crew, and make sure that safety practices are followed at all times. On freight trains, conductors take responsibility for all freight and maintain schedules and switching orders so that individual cars get to where they need to go.

Yardmasters

As the name implies, yardmasters are in charge of entire rail yards. They move the pieces around. They know where every car is at any given moment. They know what is on the trains coming in and what needs to be on the trains going out. They direct rail yard engineers to make it all happen. Without yardmasters trains could not be configured correctly.

Yardmasters use computers to track cars and locomotives. Many yards also feature big-screen maps of the yard and all the sidings in it that allow the yardmaster to assess the state of the yard at a glance. It takes more than computers to master a busy rail yard, however. Yardmasters have many years of experience and an intimate knowledge of the rail business and of their yard. They learn how to achieve maximum efficiency at all times.

Brake Operators

Brake operators are in charge of coupling and uncoupling cars. They work mostly in rail yards but sometimes travel with a train crew. This is extremely hands-on work.

Train braking systems are very complex. Amazingly, the air-brake system in use today is a direct descendant of the system patented by George Westinghouse in 1868. The system is still known as the Westinghouse system to this day. The system uses air reservoirs on each car to create a pressurized system throughout the entire length of the train. Brake operators have to connect the brake hoses whenever they couple cars together. The entire system has to be pressurized before the train can pull away.

Interestingly, the Westinghouse system does not engage the brakes when pressure is applied to the brakes, but when pressure is reduced. This innovation was critical. Earlier braking systems applied pressure to engage the brakes. This worked fine until a line broke and the system lost pressure. Without pressure the train would run away, unable to be stopped. When trains equipped with a Westinghouse system lose pressure they come to a stop – a much safer method. Brake operators are responsible for making sure this critical system is always in working order.

Signal Operators

Signal operators are responsible for signals in rail yards and along tracks. Even in the digital age old-fashioned signals play an important role in moving trains around safely. They can tell a locomotive engineer or rail yard engineer what is up ahead at a glance. Signals work the same way as street signs. When you see a red octagon, you stop. You do not take the time to read the sign because you know what it means at a glance.

Switch Operators

Switch operators control switches in rail yards. Switches are what enable trains to move onto different tracks. As efficient as they may be out on the open rails, trains are notoriously difficult to move around when in the yard. Unlike trucks or automobiles they cannot simply steer from one track to another. That is the purpose of switches. Many yards have adopted computerized switches that can be controlled by a yardmaster or by a switch operator who does most of the job from an office.

Mechanical Careers

Railroads employ many careerists in maintenance and mechanical positions that keep the trains running. A few community colleges offer two-year programs in railroad mechanics, but most railroads offer in-house training programs for promising applicants. Mechanics work in huge buildings often known as sheds or roundhouses. They repair locomotives and rolling stock when they break and conduct routine maintenance to prevent wear and tear, and maximize efficiency.

Engineering Careers

Railroads need civil engineers to build and maintain the extensive infrastructure needed to keep the system moving along. Trains are not worth much without tracks, and tracks do not build themselves. Tracks also need to be laid in places that are not necessarily flat and featureless. Building bridges and tunnels is a complex process. So is grading land and carving out the sides of mountains to create a slot for a right-of-way. Sometimes it takes decades to lay a few miles of track to a new location.

RAILROAD PROS TELL THEIR OWN STORIES

I Am a Locomotive Engineer for a Freight Railroad

"I have the best job in the railroad business. I am a locomotive engineer for a major freight railroad. Yes, I really do wear the traditional striped cap.

I started my career after high school. I got a job as a signal switcher at a rail yard not far from my home. The training was extremely rigorous. I took a few written exams but spent most of my time out in the yard working alongside veteran signal switchers. There was a lot to learn and exactly zero margin for error. Trains are guided by switches in the tracks. One mistake can result in disaster.

After a few years I decided that I really wanted to ride the trains. I loved the railroad business. Its legacy is everywhere, from the traditional clothing and language to the pride everybody takes in their job. Everybody in this business knows a lot about railroading history. I can't think of another industry in which so many people know so much about their shared past.

So I got myself onto the engineer track, so to speak. I had to start from the bottom with training but I progressed rapidly because I had already been in the railroad business for several years and certainly knew a lot about switching. I had to pass an extensive certification process administered by the railroad in conjunction with the Federal Railroad Administration, or FRA. The FRA runs the certification programs for both engineers and conductors. They let the railroads devise their own training programs as long as they conform to the FRA's standards.

I love my job for a lot of reasons. The best part is that I know that I'm playing a critical role in the flow of commerce across the country and around the world. Americans could not enjoy the high standard of living that we do without railroads. The work I do makes me a pivotal player in the global economy. I also appreciate railroading's legacy and its role in building America. Most industries would love to have a legacy like that. I also like to drive trains. It sounds simple, but it's true. There are few things I enjoy as much as driving a train through the countryside, winding around glorious mountains and admiring the scenery – all with thousands of tons of freight in tow. It is nothing if not invigorating.

I'd recommend this career to anybody who wants to work hard and take pride in doing their part for the American way of life. There aren't too many professions that are so closely bound up with the overall health of the country. In that sense, railroading is tough to beat."

I Am a Conductor for Amtrak

"I have the classic railroad job. I'm a conductor for Amtrak, the only long-haul rail passenger service in the United States. My job used to be quite common, back in the day when most people took trains to travel long distances. There aren't very many of us left today but what we do is critical to the functioning of the railroad.

I got into this business almost by accident. I majored in English in college. That's the major for people who don't know what they want to be when they grow up. Nothing wrong with that, though. I'm a good communicator and literary analysis fine-tuned my analytical skills. I was drawn to a career in railroading by a romantic vision, as much as anything. I had spent some time in Europe in college and rode trains everywhere. Trains are still the dominant form of long-distance travel in Europe. They're not as fast as planes but they take you from one city center directly to another city center. You don't have to arrive hours in advance and go through long security lines, either. And you get to see what's in-between. That's the best part.

So I signed on with Amtrak as an assistant conductor trainee. I worked alongside veteran conductors, which was the best way to learn. Most trains run with a conductor and an assistant conductor. The job is pretty much the same, but the conductor is ultimately the one who takes responsibility for everything. That's important.

Many people think all I do is take tickets and chat with customers. Not true. I'm responsible for managing the train. I supervise all of the employees on the train, make sure safety procedures are followed, keep track of baggage, mail and special shipments, and generally make sure that everything works the way it's supposed to. It's a big job and I love every minute of it.

I've worked in several parts of the country. In the Midwest, where routes are long, I usually stay overnight at the end of a run and come home on the return train the next day. Nowadays, I work in the densely populated Northeast Corridor, the area stretching from Washington, DC in the south, to Boston in the north. About one-seventh of Americans live in this corridor, which is Amtrak's busiest region by far. There are several big, important cities in relatively close proximity, including Washington, Baltimore, Philadelphia, Newark, New York City, Hartford, Providence and Boston.

The Northeast Corridor is the only part of the Amtrak system that makes money. A lot of people see Amtrak as a failure because it requires a public subsidy from taxpayers in order to make ends meet. I see their point, but in the grand scheme of things Amtrak's subsidy is minuscule. All those European train systems that American tourists think are so great are heavily subsidized by their governments. They are investments that allow their citizens to get around and conduct business. Business is where the taxes come from. I don't see a problem with that."

I Am a Yardmaster

"Yardmasters are responsible for managing rail yards. We are like conductors for the yards. We don't ride the trains. Only the largest rail yards have full-time yardmasters. Smaller yards and spurs use conductors to do the job. When a yard needs a yardmaster you know it's a busy place.

My most important job is keeping track of the rolling stock. We have locomotives, empty cars, and cars filled with freight. They are in constant motion. Rail yard engineers drive dinkeys around the yard to pull cars onto sidings and into position to be coupled into trains. I direct all of this activity.

You may think that trains just chug across the country from origin to destination, maybe making a few stops along the way to switch crews. It's a lot more complicated than that. When an east-west train rolls into a major yard, for example, it may have to be broken up into several smaller units. Some cars may keep going in the original direction, but others may need to go north or south, and there may be cars sitting on sidings that need to go back where the train came from. Cars have to be coupled together into completely new trains, locomotives have to be added and crews switched. Empty cars may need to be coupled to trains to pick up freight at a faraway destination that doesn't have enough empty cars. The parade of switching orders and shipping records never ends. This is logistics in its purest form.

I began my career after high school as a switch operator. I earned an associate degree in railroad operations after I had been in the business for a few years because I knew that I wanted to move into the more complex part of the business. I'm glad I did. This is a seniority-driven business. I would probably have been able to make the switch to yardmastering eventually but earning the degree put me at the top of the list of candidates. It's a fascinating job."

I Am a Rail Yard Engineer

"I drive trains but I rarely leave the rail yard. I'm a rail yard engineer, one of the people responsible for making sense out of the chaotic places known as rail yards.

A busy rail yard can have hundreds of sidings and switches. Switches allow trains to roll from one track onto another, often onto a siding, which is a length of track that runs alongside the main track and gives rolling stock a place to park while waiting to be coupled to another train. To most people a typical rail yard looks like a maze of rails and switches. They're basically right, but somebody has to make sense of it all. That's my job.

I drive small locomotives known as dinkeys. Dinkeys are powerful enough to move a few cars at a time but are small enough – hence the name – to not take up too much space around the yard. I move cars onto sidings and pull them off to couple to new trains. Each car has a final destination, so I have to make sure I get it right. If a car goes to the wrong destination, which happens, it can take days to get it back. I couple cars together that are headed for the same place so that I can move around multiple cars at once. Moving each car separately would take a lot of time and be even more confusing than it already is. I also drive full-sized locomotives around the yard and into the maintenance shops, but I never take them out of the yard.

I started this career right out of high school. I grew up near a rail yard and always thought it would be cool to work in one. I went through the company's in-house training program to become a switch operator and then moved into rail yard engineering after a few years. This job is never boring, I can tell you that. The hours aren't always the best. Sometimes I work nights for a few weeks and barely see my kids. When I get enough seniority I'll only have to work day shifts, however. It's a pretty good deal."

I Am an Engineer for a Railroad

"When I tell people that I'm an engineer for a railroad they immediately think that I'm a locomotive engineer. Nope. I'm an engineer-engineer. I have a Master of Science degree in civil engineering. I could have done a lot of things with my education but I chose to go into railroading.

When you talk to most people about railroads the first thing they think of is a train. That's understandable, but trains without tracks wouldn't be very useful. Tracks without bridges and tunnels wouldn't do anybody any good. Nothing would go anywhere without regarding the countryside. I'm the person who gets to do it all.

You've undoubtedly seen movies in which a railroad bridge gets blown up, causing a train to plunge to its fiery demise. As a civil engineer it is my job to build and maintain the infrastructure that keeps the trains running the way they're supposed to. My bridges don't blow up.

I work for a major freight railroad. We have lines crisscrossing the country. They cross hundreds of bridges, glide through almost as many tunnels and snake their way through mountains. Have you ever considered what it takes to get a mile-long freight train around a tight bend, into a tunnel and into another bend on the other side? All while maintaining a steady speed? I get to consider this stuff every day.

A lot of our infrastructure is very old. Our company dates to the middle of the 19th century and our rolling stock still runs on the same right-of-way granted by the federal government. Most of the track has been replaced several times, but staying on top of the natural wear and tear is a never-ending process. There are also new construction techniques, new materials and whole new technologies to think about, along with new federal regulations that often dictate how and why we conduct maintenance or make new investments. I love my job because it gives me almost limitless opportunities to ply my trade as a civil engineer. I get to work on a wide variety of projects, often in interesting places. My work has an immediate effect upon the lives of millions of people."

PERSONAL QUALITIES REQUIRED

TO SUCCEED IN THE RAILROAD BUSINESS you need to have some special personal traits. Most importantly, you need to be a good team player. No single person runs a train or a rail yard. Although automation plays a bigger role today, trains and rail yards still depend upon human judgment and interaction in order to operate at maximum efficiency. Human error can be catastrophic. Conductors, engineers, brake operators, switch operators and signal operators need to be in constant contact with one another, and everybody needs to know exactly what to do and when to do it. This high degree of teamwork is absolutely crucial to the success of any railroad. A major freight railroad, for example, may have several thousand cars crisscrossing the country at any one time. Many cars need to be uncoupled when they get to particular hubs so that they can be coupled to different trains headed for other destinations. Enormous containers need to be lifted from arriving trucks and positioned perfectly on waiting flatbed cars, while other containers need to be unloaded from trains and placed on waiting trucks for intermodal transport direct to the door of shippers. Empty cars are uncoupled and then moved onto sidings to wait for the next train. This process is incredibly complex, must happen in perfect sequence in rail yards hundreds or thousands of miles apart, and never, ever stops. To succeed in this career you must be a reliable team player.

That means you need to have excellent communications skills. Take a trip to a rail yard or even just a rail junction. You will see many signal lights and other communications devices meant to relay important messages to engineers. These devices came into use long before the advent of the radio and text-based communications systems used today. They still work, and give engineers a clear picture of what is ahead. Signal failure is one of the leading causes of train wrecks. Engineers need to know to anticipate what's ahead on the tracks, and accurate and prompt communications will be required.

The need to be physically fit cannot be overstated. Rail yards and rolling stock are dangerous. A typical rail car weighs many tons and runs on heavy steel wheels with flanges that can cut anything in two. Rail yards tend to be crowded, restraining visibility. You need to be able to move quickly and confidently across the yard. You will also need to be able to climb ladders and lift heavy objects. If you pursue a career as a mechanic you will find yourself bending, stretching and lifting all day, every day.

ATTRACTIVE FEATURES

THERE ARE MANY THINGS TO LIKE about a career in railroading. Railroads are absolutely essential to commerce and the American way of life. Railroads are the least expensive way to move heavy freight over long distances. On average, it costs about five cents to move a ton of freight one mile by rail. That works out to about 12 cents to move an automobile one mile, or only $120 to move it 1,000 miles. By comparison, it costs about 50 cents to move a ton of freight one mile by truck and about five dollars to move the same ton by air! Ships, which are necessary to move freight across the oceans, cost about 10 cents per ton. Railroads are by far the least expensive.

Railroads are also a critical part of the global containerized shipping system. An essential function of worldwide commerce, containerized shipping uses standardized containers to move just about everything. Containers are large rectangular steel boxes that look like truck trailers without the wheels, which is essentially what they are. To illustrate, a factory in Taiwan fills a container with bicycles and puts the container on a truck. The truck takes the container on a short trip to the nearest shipping port. There, it is offloaded from the truck and lifted onto an enormous container vessel along with hundreds or even thousands of other similar containers. The ship then sails across the Pacific Ocean to a port on the West Coast of the United States. The container is offloaded onto a truck for a short trip to the nearest rail hub, or possibly loaded directly onto a flatcar of a train that has pulled alongside the port. The container then crosses the United States by train until it gets to its market in, say, Chicago. There, it is once again lifted onto a truck for the last leg of its journey to a bike distributor, big box store, or retail bike shop. Every day containers make millions of these journeys around the world, bringing goods to the people who want them. Railroads are essential partners in this process.

Jobs are very stable. This is primarily because of two factors. First, railroading is a heavily unionized business in which it is difficult to fire someone. Second, the jobs that remain after decreases in recent years are essential to the functioning of the system. They require a high degree of skill, and they are jobs to take pride in. Turnover in the railroad business is very low compared to most other occupations. Getting your foot in the door may take some effort, but once you are in, you should be able to stay.

You can see the spirit whenever you are around railroad people. Conductors often sport handlebar mustaches redolent of days gone by. Engineers wear striped caps that have not changed in more than a century. Railroad companies maintain a steam engine or two and bring them out for special occasions. Few industries revel in their history the way railroading does. American history textbooks stress the importance of railroads in opening up the American West. Railroads have been immortalized in movies and songs. They are inseparable from a romantic vision of our past.

UNATTRACTIVE ASPECTS

MOST RAILROAD CAREERS COME WITH schedules that can be taxing on you and your family. Railroading is a 24/7/365 operation. Trains never stop, so neither do the people who make them run. While most shifts may be during regular daytime working hours, not all of them are. Somebody has to be on duty at all times. More often than not, it is the junior employees who work the odd hours while their senior colleagues get to go home at night. Railroading is very hierarchical, and senior employees almost always get to pick their shifts. Some railroad jobs require employees to leave home for days or even weeks at a time. Engineers and conductors, in particular, have to go wherever the trains go. If that means a cross-country journey lasting several days you had better be willing to pack your bags. This may not seem like a problem right now, but the day may come when you have a family to think about. They will probably prefer to have you around as often as possible.

Railroading can be dangerous. Serious accidents are few and far between only because safety is drilled into everybody all the time. Safety briefings and training sessions are routine and required by company policy and federal law. Rail yards also conduct emergency training with local first providers like police and fire departments. The need for constant communications and teamwork is stressed in everything railroads do, but when accidents do happen they can be disastrous. Derailments can result in multiple injuries and deaths. Derailments involving dangerous cargo, like tanker cars filled with toxic chemicals, may require the evacuation of nearby areas. Bridge failures or switching mistakes that lead to collisions are always deadly. Relatively minor injuries like broken bones, joint injuries, and bumps and bruises are very common.

The railroad business is shrinking. Not in terms of the number of miles traveled or tons carried but in the number of people working for railroads. Railroading was once one of the largest employers in the United States. Today only about 115,000 people work for railroads, and that number is expected to drop to about 110,000 within the coming decade. Automation is the prime factor behind the drop in railroad jobs. Computers can do many jobs better and more cost-effectively than humans can. The upside to this reality is that the jobs that remain require more skills than ever. The human element has an important place in railroading, and probably always will.

EDUCATION AND TRAINING

BEYOND A HIGH SCHOOL DIPLOMA, there are no formal educational requirements to get into the railroad business. Railroad companies maintain their own training programs and administer certification exams in conjunction with the Federal Railroad Administration (FRA). The main exception to this rule applies to railroad engineers. Some mechanical careers also require formal education beyond high school.

Generally speaking, new railroad employees choose this

career path and enter their employer's in-house training program. Railroad training programs are very rigorous and require new hires to spend long days working under the watchful eyes of experienced senior employees. Safety depends upon everybody in the organization being on the same page all the time. On-the-job training, or OJT, is the backbone of railroad training programs.

Engineers and conductors must be certified by the FRA. Certification is an arduous process that consists of OJT and written exams administered by the employer in compliance with standards enforced by the FRA. Training typically lasts for several months and is followed by a probationary period in which the new careerist is carefully supervised by a senior colleague.

A small number of community colleges offer associate degree programs in railroad operations. These degrees require courses in field operations, railroad history, railroad safety, and basic technical training. A degree in railroad operations is not required for entry into this profession but earning one will definitely give you an advantage in getting hired and learning your new trade.

Careerists pursuing mechanical careers should set their sights on earning associate degrees in mechanical engineering technology. Typical curricula include sections devoted to basic mechanical concepts, materials and metallurgy, advanced mathematics, and practical exercises like working in an auto shop.

College may not be absolutely necessary to get into this business, but it can definitely accelerate your career progress. College also offers other opportunities to broaden your horizons. Chief among these opportunities is the ability to complete an internship. Simply stated, an internship is a full-time job related to your major that takes the place of classes for a summer or semester. Most internships are paid, and all come with opportunities to do things that most employees don't get to do, like getting specialized training. Never again in your career will you have such an opportunity to try on a career for size and then walk away after a few months without burning your bridges behind you. You may make a lot of coffee but time spent in the company of working professionals will teach you about what to expect when you get your first job after school. Best of all, many careerists get their first real jobs after school with the companies where they completed their internships. You will make connections and have a much easier time of getting your career off the ground than you will if you do not seize the opportunity for an internship.

Do you need to set your sights on higher education? Earning a bachelor's degree will definitely give you a competitive advantage when looking for a job. It will also give you a competitive advantage as you move up the ladder with your employer. Careerists who aspire to become railroad engineers – not locomotive engineers, but railroad engineers – should definitely earn degrees in civil engineering. Railroad companies employ people with general business skills, too. Earning a bachelor's degree in business administration or supply-chain management while you are working in the rail yard could put you in the running for the kind of corporate job you may never have thought about before.

Think about a hitch in the military. None of the armed services operate railroads but they all depend upon them to move things around. More importantly, all of the services offer outstanding training programs in logistics and supply-chain management, which are what railroads do. Some railroads prefer to hire veterans because they know that veterans can handle major responsibilities. One five-year hitch in the military will give you training and experience that your competitors will not have.

EARNINGS

EARNINGS VARY IN THE RAILROAD industry, but just about any career path you choose will provide you with a comfortable living. Add to that the stability and full slate of fringe benefits that come with railroad careers and you have a very nice package.

Railroad conductors and yardmasters earn about $60,000 per year. Locomotive engineers are paid about $55,000 per year. Brake, signal and switch operators make about $50,000 per year, and rail yard engineers, hostlers and dinkey operators earn about $45,000 per year.

Most jobs come with opportunities for overtime, which typically pays one-and-a-half times the usual hourly rate. Some employees, like engineers and conductors, are required by law to take a minimum number of rest hours in order to make sure that they are wide awake when in control of a train.

These salaries come with above-average benefits, including paid vacations and health insurance. You will not get rich in the railroad business, but you will do very well and have a career you can take pride in.

It should be noted that senior executives of railroad companies can earn hundreds of thousands of dollars per year. This report has concentrated on careers specifically involved in railroading, as opposed to more general managerial careers. Still, nothing says you cannot earn a Master of Business Administration degree and set your sights on an executive position with a rail company.

One opportunity railroads do not offer very much is entrepreneurial opportunity. The barriers to entry – the amount of money needed to get into the game – are just too high. Most railroads can trace their origins to generous federal land grants of the 1800s that gave railroad companies huge tracts of land in order to get started. Those tracts were oddly shaped, to be sure, sometimes consisting of little more than a narrow right-of-way stretching for hundreds of miles. Some modern commentators have argued that railroad companies should be required to pay the government for its long-ago largesse but that will not happen. The railroads got free land, but what they did with that land created vast new wealth and American opportunity.

OPPORTUNITIES

THERE ARE MANY WAYS TO GET ahead in the railroad business. Railroading is not easy work. Hours can be long, work can be hazardous, if not outright dangerous, and schedules can be less-than-ideal. If you want to get ahead, volunteer for the hard jobs. Managers remember who stepped up when times were tough. Make sure that you are that person. Be the employee who comes through in the clutch, or even just the loyal person who makes the company's welfare a top priority. This is good advice for anyone, but it is especially important for those who go into demanding jobs with nontraditional hours and often hazardous working conditions. Be the one who never complains and you will go far.

Railroads keep track of everything. It is the nature of highly regulated, highly unionized businesses especially concerned with safety. In most railroad offices you will see a sign proclaiming "We've had XX days without an injury," or words to that effect. Accidents are not only harmful to people, they are harmful to the company and to its customers. Delays cost money. Broken equipment costs money. Injuries not only cost money but also may change lives, and not for the better. Accidents and mistakes are logged.

Earning extra credentials will help promote your career. Some railroad companies offer management-training opportunities to employees with a bachelor's degree. Usually, you have to spend a few years working in operations before you can look to get into a management position. If you have a bachelor's degree you can sometimes skip the line entirely, and head right into a managerial job. If you are already working in the railroad business you can make yourself more competitive by earning a degree.

GETTING STARTED

WHEN THE TIME COMES TO GET YOUR first real job after you finish school, you want to make sure to put your best foot forward. You owe it to yourself to think about this before you leap into the first job that comes along. Prepare your personal marketing materials. Fill out every application you can get your hands on.

Personal marketing materials are critical to making a good first impression. You may or may not need a cover letter but you will definitely need a résumé. Most of the applications you fill out will be online. You may never use a résumé formatted in the traditional way. It is still recommended that you write a traditional résumé, however. Even if you do not ever send the full printed résumé to anybody you will be able to cut and paste paragraphs from your résumé into online applications. This saves the hassle of writing the same material over and over, and keeps you consistent from one application to the next. Tweaking your credentials to say what you think a particular employer wants to hear is the kind of tactic that can come back to haunt you. Resist the urge to embellish. There are numerous software applications and books available to help you craft a perfect résumé. Take advantage of them.

If you have connections in the railroad business as a result of an internship, get in touch with them. You might be surprised by what they can offer you. Even if your connections do not have any jobs to offer they may know somebody who does. Unless a job falls into your lap you should plan on filling out every application you can find. This will mean going online and looking up the career pages of every railroad company in your area. Fill out their online applications, cutting and pasting from your résumé, until you have made the rounds of all of them. Railroads have very regimented hiring processes that may take a few months. Do not expect instant results.

Keep an open mind. You may have your sights set on becoming a conductor but do not be afraid to spend a few years in some other department, like switching or engineering. Turnover in the railroad business is very low. Many employees stay in railroading for the their entire working lives. This means that the job you want may not be available until somebody retires and allows other people to move up a notch, creating an opportunity for you. Be patient, but be willing to take a job that gets your foot in the door. Then you can start accruing some seniority and be in a position to get that dream job when it comes along.

ASSOCIATIONS
PERIODICALS
WEBSITES

■ **Alaska Railroad**
www.alaskarailroad.com

■ **American Railway Development Association**
www.amraildev.com

■ **American Railway Engineering and Maintenance-of-Way Association**
www.arema.org

■ **American Short Line and Regional Railroad Association**
www.aslrra.org

■ **Amtrak**
www.amtrak.com

■ **Association of American Railroads**
www.aar.org

■ **Burlington Northern Santa Fe**
www.bnsf.com

■ **Canadian National**
www.cn.ca

■ **CSX**
www.csx.com

■ **Federal Railroad Administration**
www.fra.dot.gov

■ **Kansas City Southern**
www.kcsouthern.com

■ **Lionel**
www.lionel.com

■ **National Model Railroad Association**
www.nmra.org

■ **National Railroad Construction and Maintenance Association**
www.nrcma.org

■ **National Railway Historical Society**
www.nrhs.com

■ **Norfolk Southern**
www.nscorp.com

■ **Progressive Railroading**
www.progressiverailroading.com

■ **Rail Jobs**
www.railjobs.com

■ **Rail Personnel**
www.railpersonnel.com

■ **Railroad Data**
www.railroaddata.com

■ **Railroad Training Services**
www.railroadtrainingservices.com

■ **Railway Age**
www.railwayage.com

■ **Railway and Locomotive Historical Society**
www.rlhs.org

■ **Sterling Rail**
www.sterlingrail.com

■ **Train Web**
www.trainweb.com

■ **Union Pacific**
www.up.com

■ **Western Railway Club**
www.westernrailwayclub.com

Copyright 2015

Institute For Career Research

Website www.careers-internet.org

For information on other Careers Reports please contact

service@careers-internet.org

www.ingramcontent.com/pod-product-compliance
Lightning Source LLC
Chambersburg PA
CBHW070748180526

45168CB00004B/1563